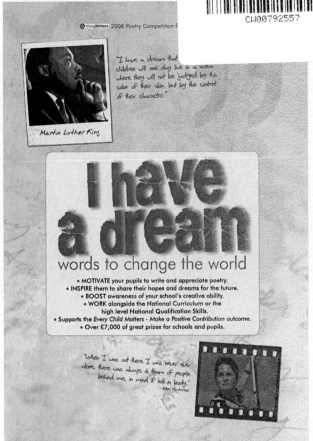

youngwriters 2006 Poetry Competition

"I have a dream that my children will one day live in a nation where they will not be judged by the color of their skin, but by the content of their character."

Martin Luther King

I have a dream

words to change the world

- MOTIVATE your pupils to write and appreciate poetry.
- INSPIRE them to share their hopes and dreams for the future.
- BOOST awareness of your school's creative ability.
- WORK alongside the National Curriculum or the high level National Qualification Skills.
- Supports the *Every Child Matters - Make a Positive Contribution* outcome.
- Over £7,000 of great prizes for schools and pupils.

"When I was out there I was never ever alone, there was always a team of people behind me, in mind if not in body."
Ellen MacArthur

Poems From Wales
Edited by Angela Fairbrace

 Young**Writers**

First published in Great Britain in 2006 by:
Young Writers
Remus House
Coltsfoot Drive
Peterborough
PE2 9JX
Telephone: 01733 890066
Website: www.youngwriters.co.uk

SB ISBN 1 84602 528 1

Foreword

Imagine a teenager's brain; a fertile yet fragile expanse teeming with ideas, aspirations, questions and emotions. Imagine a classroom full of racing minds, scratching pens writing an endless stream of ideas and thoughts . . .

. . . Imagine your words in print reaching a wider audience. Imagine that maybe, just maybe, your words can make a difference. Strike a chord. Touch a life. Change the world. Imagine no more . . .

'I Have a Dream' is a series of poetry collections written by 11 to 18-year-olds from schools and colleges across the UK and overseas. Pupils were invited to send us their poems using the theme 'I Have a Dream'. Selected entries range from dreams they've experienced to childhood fantasies of stardom and wealth, through inspirational poems of their dreams for a better future and of people who have influenced and inspired their lives.

The series is a snapshot of who and what inspires, influences and enthuses young adults of today. It shows an insight into their hopes, dreams and aspirations of the future and displays how their dreams are an escape from the pressures of today's modern life. Young Writers are proud to present this anthology, which is truly inspired and sure to be an inspiration to all who read it.

Contents

Sophie Talbot (12)	79
Kithma Welgama (14)	80
Robert Murray (13)	81
Charis Lee (12)	82
Lizzie Tavener (12)	83
Kirsty Veitch (13)	84
Josh Evans (13)	85
Zoe Griffiths (13)	86
Mercedes White (12)	87
Levi Robinson (11)	88
Beatrice Kamau (12)	89
Jack Govier (12)	90
Rachel Jones (12)	91
Nathan Holley (11)	92
Aaron Marfell (12)	93
Maya Mossop (11)	94
Harry Lesbirel (11)	95
Rhys Willbourn (11)	96
Sam Ellis (11)	97
Ryan Price (11)	98
Jack Wheatley (11)	99
Cheri Jones (14)	100
Sophie Smith (12)	101
Emma Parton-Wroe (12)	102
Tom Fury (12)	103
Isabel Anne Stokes (12)	104
Antony Symonds (12)	106
David Fury (11)	107
Ciaran Griffiths	108
Jayson Hollingworth (11)	109
Rachel Atkinson (12)	110
Nicholas Davies (12)	111
Sophie Cashell (11)	112
Lydia Nicholas (12)	113
Beth Davies	114
Catrin Menzies (11)	115
Naomi Williams (12)	116
Katie Brocklehurst (11)	117
Kieran Lewis (12)	118
Ben Jones (11)	119
Ella Parkinson (12)	120
Josh Tavener (13)	121

The Poems

I Have A Dream

I have a dream
To never grow up
To stay on Earth the way I should
To love my mum, my sister too
To plan ahead for my little brother as he grows
To watch him follow in my steps that I put there
Before I go to show him that life is hard sometimes
But tell him to follow through
That if I go, I will be there to watch him from above
To give him a shove
To never let him down
I will be there, in the sky
To watch as the clouds go by
To tell him to never lie.

Holly Jones (12)
Holywell High School, Holywell

Little Kids' Dreams

I have a dream
It is to be an astronaut
So I can fly high
And see the stars in the sky

I have a dream
It is to be a policewoman
So I can help people
Night and day

I have a dream
It is to be a dancer
So I can twist and turn
Jump and leap

I have a dream
It is to be a champion
So I can be
The best in the world

I have a dream
It is to be a fireman
So I can put out fires
And no one will get hurt

I have a dream
It is to be a friend
So I can have loads of friends
So I can be loving to them

I have a dream
It is to never grow up
Like my favourite character
Peter Pan

Now you know all about my dreams
I hope they come true one day.

Emily Seabourne (12)
Holywell High School, Holywell

I Have A Dream

I have a dream
That bullying is gone
And that people are happy
And not sad
That people can be friends
And get along happily
The world would be so much better
And people would not get hurt and injured
And children could enjoy their lives.

Lauren Jade Tancock (12)
Holywell High School, Holywell

I Have A Dream

I have a dream to stop cruelty

H oping that it will stop
A s soon as possible
V ery soon
E very night

A t

D arkness I
R emember
E vil and cruelty to
A nimals and
M ankind

I have a dream to stop cruelty.

Roxanne Bacon (12)
Holywell High School, Holywell

I Have A Dream

I have a dream
That all things are good
That animals stay cute
And no one will be bad.

I have a dream
That bullying will be gone
And people will be happy
Having loads of fun.

I have a dream
That litter will go
And people will give
More respect as they go.

Siân Ellen Hughes (12)
Holywell High School, Holywell

I Had A Dream

I had a dream of a land so pure,
With grass of every shade of green,
A sea as blue as the reflected sky,
That is what I have seen.

I had a dream of a world full of life,
Animals bustling everywhere,
The sky was bright and the clouds so white,
So clean was the air.

I had a dream of a friendly planet,
With nothing intimidating,
No one was hurt and no one was killed
And everyone liked to sing.

I had a dream of an animals' world
With animals here and there,
No one to hurt or kill them,
Everything was fair.

I had a dream of all these things,
Smoking, pollution, it's not new,
Loads and loads of other things,
Who makes a difference?
You!

Bethan Louise Price (11)
Holywell High School, Holywell

I Have A Dream

I   have a dream that

D rink driving is no more
R obbers kept well away and there's an
E nd to all wars
A buse is taken care of
M urderers put into prison

Why can't we live in a world that has no murders and crime?

If
We all
Dream
Hard enough
It might come true!

Sarah Jayne Grundy (12)
Holywell High School, Holywell

I Have A Dream

I have a dream,
Pollution, pollution,
Bad old pollution,
Noise, smell and visual pollution,
Cough, cough, don't forget air pollution,
Big, long chimneys full of smoke and pollution,
Global warming, acid rain,
Burning life and bringing pain.

Stop pollution, stop pollution,
Now, now, *now!*
If you don't, you will destroy the Earth,
Especially since it's five billions years old,
Bad pollution, bad pollution,
Stop pollution, bad pollution,
Now!

Thomas Garner (12)
Holywell High School, Holywell

I Had A Dream

I had a dream when all was dark,
The match was lit without a spark.

I had a dream of the world as it is,
Dark, polluted and all in a tizz.

I had a dream of the moon and stars,
Saturn, Jupiter, Pluto and Mars.

I had a dream of love and care,
Without all happiness the world would be bare.

I had a dream of the sea being blue,
But fortunately it's not because of all the rubbish we threw.

I had a dream of running away,
Because of the world as it is today.

Hannah Bartley (12)
Holywell High School, Holywell

I Have A Dream

I have a dream
Why, why, why do we
All have to fight?
Bang! Kaboom!
It doesn't sound right

People dying,
Families crying
Why does everyone
Have to fight?

Where would you get
By having a war?
Countries' respect,
Weapons galore,
All they do is start a war
Why? Why? Why?

Ben Hatchett (12)
Holywell High School, Holywell

I Have A Dream

I have a dream
That the world can have equal rights
And to make everything to be ozone friendly
If the world had equal rights there would be no wars,
No poverty, no crime
If everything was ozone friendly there would be no
Global warming and the Earth would be perfect
The world would be warm, have clean air and water
Nothing would be dumped into the sea
I have another dream
That there will be no bad drugs, racism and starvation
If there were no bad drugs the world would be a better place.

Callum Percival (13)
Holywell High School, Holywell

I Have A Dream

I have a dream, all the drugs are gone,
Marijuana, speed and crack,
All those people that get doped up,
End up crawling back.

The people will end up seriously ill,
But they still stay on the pill,
They have got to learn to stop taking drugs,
Or they will turn out to be the mugs.

Dylan Harris (13)
Holywell High School, Holywell

I Have A Dream

I have a dream
That white people, black people and Asian people
Can live in this world
Without being harassed or abused
Just in peace
In the words of Tupac Shakira
'It ain't about black and white, cos we human'
People should not be judged
By nationality or colour
There is no such thing
As the wrong colour
Wrong nationality
Wrong race
Although . . .
That is just a dream.

Chris Owens (12)
Holywell High School, Holywell

I Have A Dream

I have a dream,
Poverty, poverty,
Help end poverty.
Help the poor,
Get rid of diseases.

Give the children education,
Give them more food
And medicine,
Because every
Three seconds
A child dies in Africa.

Give them more money,
Help cure poverty,
Because it's just like
A disease.

Jessica Lucy Roberts (12)
Holywell High School, Holywell

I Have A Dream

To stop world poverty
We should stop the war on Iraq
Make world peace
Black and white, it does not matter, we're all human
Stop the drugs from getting into this country
Stop the fighting on the streets.

Jarrod Howarth (12)
Holywell High School, Holywell

I Have A Dream!

I have a dream,
That people can live together,
No matter what their race or beliefs,
'It ain't about black or white cos we're human'.
On the outside we look different, yeah sure,
But on the inside we're all the same,
Racism even happens in a football game.
There is no such thing as the wrong colour or nationality,
If there was, we'd all be wrong to some.
What is the point of being racist anyway?
We all like a laugh and a joke
But why be offensive?
That's my dream,
No more racism!

Jack Jones (13)
Holywell High School, Holywell

I Have A Dream

I have a dream,
That the world is clean,
No more crime,
Not as much grime.

We have world peace,
We have equal rights,
No more fights, no starvation,
End of poverty, end of disease.

Dispose of drugs,
Or you are thugs,
More food for the unable,
Cures for the disabled.

No more homelessness,
The nations are the world union,
End vandalism, end racism, end homophobia,
I have a dream, that is my dream.

Jake Harrison (12)
Holywell High School, Holywell

I Have A Dream

I have a dream,
A vision perhaps,
That the world will stop fighting,
Don't make it collapse.

I want world peace,
Let people get on,
Or the world will be gone.

Stop tearing it apart,
Racism, war, pollution,
I think I have the solution,
I have a dream.

Delyth Hughes
Holywell High School, Holywell

I Have A Dream

I have a dream
That the world is clean,
No more fighting
And no more war,
The world
Has less poor.

We have world peace,
No more homeless,
More money,
More food.

No more crimes,
No more drugs,
No more vandalism
And no more diseases,
That's my dream.

Sam Leahy (12)
Holywell High School, Holywell

I Have A Dream!

I have a dream,
That there is no war
And that someone special
Will appear at your door.

I have a dream,
That there is no bad
To be evil in this world
You must be mad.

I have a dream,
That everything is good
Although it's a bad little world
Improve it, we could.

I have a dream,
Just the same as you
Hopefully,
It will come true!

Eliot Davies (13)
Holywell High School, Holywell

I Have A Dream!

I have a dream,
For nothing bad to be seen,
To stop bullying and war,
All the things we don't care for.

I wish so hard, I wish so much,
All these things I could clutch,
I'd open the window and throw them out,
Gone are the things we worry about!

I have a dream to be in the mood,
To help everyone, give the homeless food,
But for now I'd like to stay in my room
And stare at the world that's full of gloom.

I wish someone else could have my dream,
To be like me, to be so keen,
To help the world and hold the key,
To the end of starvation and poverty.

As I'm walking down the street,
I see homeless with bare, bleeding feet,
I wish I could give them food and water
And stop them being a volunteer for slaughter.

I wish so many different things,
From no global warming, to us all having wings,
But right now, I wish most of all,
For there to be no bad and for us to stand tall!

Sophie Pritchard (12)
Holywell High School, Holywell

I Have A Dream

I have a dream
Of no poverty or war
I have a dream
That nobody's poor anymore.

I have a dream
Of no bullying at all
Just a male bird
Awaiting a female's call.

Maybe our world
Should change
Start a new book
Turn to the next page.

Amy Smith (12)
Holywell High School, Holywell

I Have A Dream

I have a dream to change the world
Stand by the sea and look,
Stop all the bad things happening
And start a new, fresh book.

All the things I'd like to change,
Like poverty and war,
Store bad things in the closet
And quickly shut the door.

I would stop all the bullies
And send them far away,
I'd try to cure illness
As people do today.

All the things I'd like to change,
Impossible as they sound,
Many people have tried these things,
To my knowledge, I have found.

All these things I wish upon,
As I dream away at night,
The closet door is finally shut
And now I see the light.

Rebecca Corfield
Holywell High School, Holywell

I Have A Dream

I have a dream,
As I walk through the door,
They take my bag off me
And chuck it on the floor.

They thump me and kick me,
My arm is all bruised,
But so is my knee,
There's nothing to lose.

I stumble to class
And sit on my own,
They blame things on me,
I get kicked if I moan.

My friends say, 'Report them,'
So that's what I'll do,
I tell my form teacher,
But what can she do?

At last things are better,
The boys have moved school,
They've walked out the door
And I'm bullied no more.

I sometimes think back to
The days that I'd scream,
A world without bullies,
That's what I dream.

Ellie Weaver (12)
Holywell High School, Holywell

I Have A Dream

I have a dream to be:
A doctor, a nurse, a vet and more,
Maybe I could go ahead and have a career in law.

I have a dream to be:
A chef, a painter, a designer and more,
Maybe I could be a teacher, but I'm not really sure.

I have a dream to be:
An inventor, a hairdresser, a singer and more,
But if I had all these jobs, it would be a bit of a chore!

Rebecca Pritchard (12)
Holywell High School, Holywell

I Have A Dream

I have a dream
And it doesn't matter who you are
Everyone's a shining star
It doesn't matter if you're black or white
It's really, really bad to fight.

It doesn't matter where you're from
So don't blow up like a bomb
It doesn't matter if you're black or white
It's really, really bad to fight.

It doesn't matter what your skin colour's like
Everyone should be liked
It doesn't matter if you're black or white
And it's really, really sad to fight.

Charlotte Appleton (13)
Holywell High School, Holywell

I Have Dreams

I have dreams

H eavenly wishing all night long
A ngels singing a sleepy song
V isible dreams that I can see
E ach and every one is here with me

D arkness hits, I go to bed
R est with dreams inside my head
E yes go drifting off to sleep
A ll my dreams I want to keep
M y memories here as it seems
S leeping and thinking, that's my dreams.

Chantelle Bennett (13)
Holywell High School, Holywell

I Have A Dream

I have a dream to help the people
To help them remember their past
If they have Alzheimer's
Every memory could be their last
They forget nearly everything
They forget their family and friends
That's why I want to help them so much
And try to make amends.

Samantha Jayne Reid (13)
Holywell High School, Holywell

I Have A Dream

I have a dream
For no more wars
Make it a law

I have a dream
For no more killing
Because life is for living

I have a dream
For no more poverty
So give them more money

I have a dream
For no more drugs
So we can have more hugs

I have a dream
For no more deforestation
So let's become a recycling nation

I have a dream
For no more racism
And less terrorism

I have a dream
For no more child abuse
For which there is no excuse

I have a dream
And that dream is
For more peace and love
In the world.

Naomi Wynn (13)
Holywell High School, Holywell

I Have A Dream

I have a dream
About my family
All sitting around
Happy as can be.

But that was until
My mum got sick
And then worst of all
My friends took the mick.

Then my mum got treatment
She lost all her hair
Dad tried to soothe me
Mum didn't care.

Mum's trying hard
Though she's lost her smile
She waits around the hospital
She stays there a while.

Now one year later
I'm crying in my bed
Dad's broke the news
Mum is now dead.

All the times we spent
The memories will remain
Although it's not that bad
I will see her again.

I have a dream
About my family
All sitting around
Happy as can be . . .

Katherine Hogarth (13)
Holywell High School, Holywell

I Have A Dream

I have a dream,
My dream is for peace to be,
A soul living in you and me,
For peace to be a part of us,
The love will travel, like the dust,
The dust travels like a cloud,
Floating, floating, floating down.

Holly Lissaman (12)
Holywell High School, Holywell

I Have A Dream

I have a dream that the world is full of peace,
No war, no fighting, no killing at least,
I dream that we all will have better lives
And that we all will be husbands and wives.

I dream that the people will all be nice
And not juggle around like little dice,
I dream that we can all be friends,
So we don't run around in awkward bends.

'I have a dream' is a famous saying,
The man was Martin Luther King,
The dream came true and so could yours,
If you just believe and say it's yours.

Lauren Smith (12)
Holywell High School, Holywell

I Have A Dream

I have a dream
About a war
And everything
Is filled with gore

I have a dream
For world peace
Where countries get along
With one another

I have a dream
About a needless war
People dying here and there
And it looks bad everywhere!

Joe Travers (12)
Holywell High School, Holywell

I Have A Dream

I have a dream
That I would love to come true
All day, all night, I think about the flu

Homeless people, sitting on the street
Begging for money or a cosy seat

End to poverty in the streets
I hope black and white get to meet

End to diseases, vandalism, drugs
No more racism, pollution or thugs

No more starvation, but more police
All my dreams are about world peace.

David Riley (12)
Holywell High School, Holywell

I Have A Dream

I have a dream
To be a mechanic
And soup-up cars for a living
And have a farm with land
To do this I'll have to work hard
And hopefully I'll make it.
I shall have some money
To put in an account for my children
Even then I will want to help
Children in Africa and help the RSPCA
To rescue poor, sick animals.

David Connaughton (12)
Holywell High School, Holywell

I Have A Dream

I dream of things when I'm in bed,
A million thoughts in my head
And snuggled up asleep and curled,
I dream, what if I ruled the world.

I'd dream I'd make a better life,
Without any struggle, stress or strife,
The only weapons would be our word
And every voice I'd make be heard.

I'd banish every bomb and gun
And unite the world into one,
No more fighting, no more war,
Just love and peace from shore to shore.

There would be no more bullies in the school
And all the teachers would be super cool
And all the orphans alone and sad,
Would all have a mum and dad.

I'd heal the sick and feed the poor
And poverty would be no more,
A cool place so it would seem,
But it's not real, it's just my dream.

I dream a dream, let's hope one day,
My dream comes true in every way,
Because it's as easy as can be,
My dream begins with you and me.

So when you snuggle down tonight,
Safe and warm, with eyes shut tight,
Dream my dream and you will see,
A better world for you and me.

This is my dream, what's yours?

Jade Woodhouse (12)
King Henry VIII School, Abergavenny

I Can't Quite Believe

I can't quite believe there's a child in my bed
I call out her name but she won't lift her head
Disease killed her mother and now this one's dead
I can't quite believe all the blood that's been shed

I can't quite believe that there's dirt in this drink
This dirt that could kill me, I can't bear to think
It's murdered the masses, the bodies all stink
The people keep drinking, communities shrink

I can't quite believe there's a gun in my hand
I'm only a child and I don't understand
It's all that I know, I grew up in this band
We kill over race, we kill over land

I can't quite believe all the food on these trees
It grows in our gardens, then sails overseas
The truth has no logic, but nobody sees
We die of starvation as well as disease

I can't quite believe that you turn out your light
You get into bed and sleep well tonight
Your comfortable life keeps on going despite
The fact that you know that the world isn't right.

Genni Jones (15)
King Henry VIII School, Abergavenny

Here And There

So thirsty
'No, this is for Papa,'
She drags the holey pail
Past heavily-laden mules
Over the sand
To her doorstep
And resisting the urge,
She hands the lifeline
To Mama.
Mama sighs at the half-empty bucket
Of dank water,
Gives it to the dying man,
Lying on the thin bed
He savours every drop
Before shutting his eyes on the world.

Disaster!
Her outfit's ready,
But she doesn't have a boyfriend
To dance to her heart's content
At the disco.
While all her friends
Flirt with their boyfriends
And have a good time
Tomorrow.
Eyes shut and head on hands, she daydreams of him -
The one.
Her mobile rings, she answers,
Listens to his question,
Smiles happily and replies
With an answer that will change her life.

Two girls
Two worlds.
Different lives
Different dreams.
If only love ruled everywhere
If only equality reigned.

Susy Stark (15)
King Henry VIII School, Abergavenny

I Have A Dream

I step out of my limousine
See the crystal sky
Reach out for my Gucci glasses
Feel like I could fly.

People all around me
Stop to look and stare
Cameras flashing, people shouting
As I flick my golden hair.

Walking down the catwalk
Feeling like a queen
Happiness is overflowing in me
As I step into the scene.

I hear a distant melody
Open up my eyes
Six o'clock, the morning's come
Now that would be the life.

Hannah Jayne Prothero (13)
King Henry VIII School, Abergavenny

I Have A Dream

Hurting yet feeling nothing,
My delicate, subtle illusion.
Flailing wildly, gasping for air,
While drowning in rippled confusion.

Breathing deep my sweetest angel,
Holding tight that hand of bliss.
Pouring out my soul, my sorrow,
Into the deep pool of cannabis.

Reaching out they call and cry,
Silence, then voices, then screaming.
Dusky twilight can only mean,
More fitful, hurtful dreaming.

My angel's gone and in her place,
The hard, masked face of the paranoid.
Left alone now, cold and distant,
Cast out to the nearing, infinite void.

Crawling softly, moving slowly,
Crying for the eternally neurotic.
Closing in, the cool, white hollow,
Home to the elusive psychotic.

Afterwards the memory haunts me
And still I feel some faint disdain.
My surface shows a lively youth,
Yet inside, no change, I feel the same.

The search for my life begins once more,
Subdued, lacks conviction and no self-esteem.
That it did not happen, that I was not there,
That will forever remain my dream.

Hannah Burch (16)
King Henry VIII School, Abergavenny

I Have A Dream

I have a dream
Playing for Man U
Having lots of money
Everything to do
Winning all the cups
Whole life ahead of you.

Sharing the good and the bad
Sharing the happy and the sad
Knowing when the manager and captain
Are very, very mad
And finally becoming
The captain!
This is my dream.

Sean Ciaren Lee (12)
King Henry VIII School, Abergavenny

I Have A Dream

Imagine
Thousands of lives wasted
Because of no food or drink
Imagine
People being killed
For just a country's pride
Imagine
One voice could change
One voice could save thousands of lives
Imagine
You were that one voice
That you could change the world
Just imagine . . .

Owain Davies (12)
King Henry VIII School, Abergavenny

I Have A Dream

Imagine . . .
Walking on a rainbow

Imagine . . .
Singing on a star

Imagine . . .
A world with no wars

Imagine . . .
Standing on the moon

Imagine . . .
Jumping out of a plane

Imagine . . .
Flying on the clouds

That's my dream!

Louis Evans (12)
King Henry VIII School, Abergavenny

I Have A Dream!

I have a dream that I'll change the world,
End hunger, poverty and even war,
Spread not pollution but
Peace, all over the world.

I have a dream that I'll soar up high,
Soar with the birds who fly in the sky,
Fly with the majestic eagle,
Fly with all birds high in the sky.

I have a dream of space exploration,
Exploring deep outer space,
The universe, the Milky Way
And everything in existence.

I have a dream that no one's afraid,
Afraid of being themselves,
Of speaking and doing,
What they think is right.

I have a dream about my voice,
My voice that's heard in a crowd,
Heard by everyone,
All over the world.

I have a dream that I'll inspire,
Inspire people all over the world,
Inspire people with,
My inspiring words.

I have a dream of immortality,
A perfect life, riches,
Royalty, a life of perfection,
For all eternity.

I have a dream, I have a dream,
Of having a dream!

Rory Lewis Havard (13)
King Henry VIII School, Abergavenny

I Have A Dream . . .

I had a dream
About a dream
And in that dream
I saw a beam
And the beam it was so bright
I could use it as a light
If I used it as a light
It would wake me up in the night
Then I would go and read a book
And look for something to cook
I then found something to cook
And tipped it on a big cook book.

Tyler Lewis (12)
King Henry VIII School, Abergavenny

I Have A Dream

I have a dream,
In a land where grass is green and water fresh
And mountains tall and lands vast,
Where rain is constant and sunlight limited,
Where songs are sung and poems read,
Where peace and harmony is everywhere,
Where people celebrate and rejoice,
Where man stands with pride,
This is Wales,
Home of the red dragon,
Land of the Celts.

Ethan Francis (12)
King Henry VIII School, Abergavenny

I Had A Dream

I dream a dream with my eyes shut tight,
I dream this dream all through the night,
Although I know it's not real,
Like the war, the tsunami that we feel

I dream the war had never begun
I dream the football team had won
I add them up inside me head
As I lie here in my bed

I wonder why they can't be true
Wishing that for me and you
I only wish the disasters hadn't begun
Then our lives would be more fun!

I dream I could become an actor
Then I could go on X-Factor
I keep adding up inside my head
As I lie here in my bed

The list carries on and on
But I know it's all wrong
I dream that I own a shop
I dream that I become a cop

Now I know that they're not true
My secrets lie with only you
My dreams aren't real but they're not fake
They're only real before I wake

All of a sudden the dreams stop there
I wake up and see my hair
I smile a little, the world's still fun
As I wake up in the morning sun!

Hannah Jones (12)
King Henry VIII School, Abergavenny

I Have A Dream

I have a dream
That all the world
That all the world will live as one

And in my dream
Everyone
Everyone will live in peace

I have a dream
That no one
That no one will be poor

And in my dream
Poverty
Poverty will be gone

I have a dream
I dream
I dream all night

And in my dream
I dream
I dream that the world will be right.

Annabel Mills (11)
King Henry VIII School, Abergavenny

I Have A Dream

I had a dream last night
I thought it was quite good
In this dream there was a fight
And it was down the woods.

I was very scared down the woods
As there wasn't any light
A big fat guy with a black hood
Came and gave me a fright.

The big fat guy with crooked legs
Was really, really scary
He played around and made a sound
That was really, really scary.

He looked like a wolf with lots of hair
Tall, thin and very bare
Frightening anyone he sees
He even frightened me.

Down in the wood
It was really dark and misty
Feeling very cold and lonely
I wish I'd brought my friend, Tony.

He reminded me of the wolf from Red Riding Hood
All my friends thought it was good
He chased me around a tree
But then I had to go and have my tea.

So I went home, had my tea
And went to bed
And had another dream.

Sarah Keogh (12)
King Henry VIII School, Abergavenny

Cure For This Cancer!

Diagnosed with no cure,
It's a disastrous disease.
Stealing so many lives,
Help us all, please!

You never suspect,
It could happen to you.
A life-saving treatment,
Would be a dream come true.

The world becomes dimmer,
It's pulling you down.
Everything is getting to you,
You can't help but frown.

Even though times get hard,
You must stand up and fight.
With hope, support and love,
The future looks bright!

You must not forget,
Your loved ones are there.
Helping you through it,
They'll prove that they care.

A cure for this 'cancer',
Is all we will wish.
Let this dream come true,
Creating an atmosphere of bliss!

Hannah Wham (14) & Coryn Price
King Henry VIII School, Abergavenny

Dream Of A Place . . .

Dream of a place that doesn't
Kill animals for their meat.
Dream of a place where
Animals can run wild and be free.
Dream of a world
Where animals aren't hurt.
Dream of a creature that
Is amazing and colourful.
Dream of a field with
Golden trees and flowers.
Dream of a place that doesn't
Have any wars or fighting.
Dream of a place where
Everyone gets along and are friends.
Dream of child that
Is always heard.
Dream of a world where
Not a single child is hurt.
Dream of a place that
Cares for the environment better.
Dream of a solar system that
We all know about and would like to find out more about it.
Dream of this place
That could be.

Kirsten Ann Clements (12)
King Henry VIII School, Abergavenny

I Have A Dream

I have a dream
                    That the world never runs out of resources
I have a dream
                    That war and conflict cease
I have a dream
                    That earthquakes and droughts stop
I have a dream
                    That diseases are cured
I have a dream
                    That racism stops.

Arthur Williams (12)
King Henry VIII School, Abergavenny

I Have A Dream

I have a dream
The snow is like cream
Coming down through the air
It's so beautiful, you've got to stare
As it comes down, out of the sky
A snowflake lands right in your eye
It's cold, refreshing and wet on your face
On hills and mountains it looks like lace
The sun comes out, it's like sparkling glass
The view is spectacular but it won't last
The sun will melt it and make it go away
But we will have more another day.

KC Pritchard (12)
King Henry VIII School, Abergavenny

The War Dream

I have a dream the war will end
I have a dream people will not be found dead
I have a dream that people survive
I have a dream people will return alive.

Hannah Gleed (14)
King Henry VIII School, Abergavenny

I Have A Dream

I have a dream
To be a rock star
Playing all night on my guitar
Make lots of money
Buy a new car

Win over the crowd
Make Mum proud
Play at Live Eight
Make a CD
Then go and give it to the needy.

Jack Bell (14)
King Henry VIII School, Abergavenny

I Have A Dream

Do you ever feel
Like no one understands you,
No matter what you say,
No matter what you do?
It does not matter what they think,
Be who you want to be!

I have a dream
That people will learn
Not to follow others
Just because they think they're cool!

Be who you want to be,
Stand out from the crowd,
Hold your head up high,
Because you should be proud,
You are the greatest one,
Because you are yourself!

I have a dream
Of individuality
And that someday
Everyone will learn to be

Themselves.

Thomas Shankland (13)
King Henry VIII School, Abergavenny

I Have A Dream

I have a dream that when I grow up
I'll meet my prince, my knight, my love,
We'll share happy moments together
And live our life in love, forever.
We'll live in a castle, a pink one I hope
And drive around in a pumpkin, everywhere we go.
When the time is right, we'll have lots of kids
And lots of pets, cute ones, that is!
We'll be one big happy family as long as we live,
But one day, the children will start their own families,
But we'll live together, me and my prince.
My dream is quite a fairy tale really
But that doesn't matter to me,
I don't need a castle or a pumpkin car.
A few wonderful children, a man that loves me,
An ordinary house and an ordinary car,
Is all I need for my dream to come true
And for me to live my life happily.

Angharad Morgan (13)
King Henry VIII School, Abergavenny

I Have A Dream

I have a dream
To be a fashion designer

I have a dream
To fall in love

I have a dream
That one day I will make a difference

I have a dream
To own a chocolate fairy castle

I have a dream
That war will end!

Polly Stroud (13)
King Henry VIII School, Abergavenny

I Have A Dream

When I was a little boy,
I had many dreams
Now I dream to be a doctor,
I want to help other people.

I would like to travel
To poor countries,
To help the sick
And infirm.

To bring cures and good health
To those who are suffering,
To be able to give service
To those who are poor.

And give a better standard of living
To those who are suffering,
To make a difference in this dying world,
A future to those who cannot afford to lose it.

Gerard Barrientos (12)
King Henry VIII School, Abergavenny

I Have A Dream

I have a dream . . .
That peace and harmony will surround me,
Friendliness is everyone's middle name
And for war and violence to surrender.

I have a dream . . .
For poverty to end, a meal for everyone every night,
Love for those who need it, a hug for those who have no one.

I have a dream . . .
That whatever race, religion or disability, everyone will be equal
That war will cease and peace rules the world
And forgiveness to be in our hearts.

I have a dream . . .
That I could fight to make my dreams come true,
But there is only so much one person can do,
I want to change frowns into smiles,
To change tears into laughter, to change hate into love.

If everyone gets together,
They could *really come true.*

Eleanor Haslegrave (12)
King Henry VIII School, Abergavenny

Justice And Peace

I have a dream, a perfect dream
That this discrimination nation is prejudice-free,
Creed, colour or race,
We will embrace,
Everyone of every background,
From all around.

I have a dream, a perfect dream,
That poverty and slavery will soon decease,
War will have ceased,
There will be peace,
Everyone from every country,
Will be free.

Jonathan Sadler (13)
King Henry VIII School, Abergavenny

I Have A Dream

No more racists, no more hate,
Be they black or white,
Both saying, 'Alright mate!'

Crying in a corner, full of pain and shame,
That is the toll that bullying takes.

Crying through the evening,
Crying through the night,
Why, why, why do they crush him so?

I'm going to the teacher
I'm finishing this right now
Thank God he hasn't gone over the edge.

Taddy Edmondson (13)
King Henry VIII School, Abergavenny

I Have A Dream

I have a dream to fly through the clouds
I have a dream to clear the world and to see all the wonder
I have a dream to inspire the world
I have a dream to see magic places and to be on top of the world.

I have a dream to see fairy tales and my favourite place in the world
I call home sweet home
I have a dream to visit a place, the one I know that is the
Holy garden of my own.

Daniel Carlos David Davies (13)
King Henry VIII School, Abergavenny

I Have A Dream

I have a dream

H urricanes to vanish
A ftershocks to never come again
V ery hard not to ask for
E arthquakes to stop

A nd

D reams to come true
R ough to become calm
E ndings will come soon
A nd not to mention the
M oon

A nd
N othing compares to
D reams

L iving a healthy life
I n my dream I am
F inding you live on
E arth.

Kelly-Marie Auty (13)
King Henry VIII School, Abergavenny

I Have A Dream

I had a dream
Just last night

I had a dream
It must come right

I have a dream
About a beautiful light

I have a dream
About a wondrous sight

I have a dream

I have a dream
About world peace

I have a dream
I'll feel safe on the streets

I have a dream
That children of the world won't die of hunger

I have a dream
Crops won't fail

I have a dream
Of a cure for cancer and diseases

I have a dream
Of only love.

Joab Froggatt (12)
King Henry VIII School, Abergavenny

I Have A Dream

I have a dream;
No more hunger
No more war
No more sorrow
No more poor

No more destruction
No more lies
No more grieving
No more cries

A world of beauty
A world of peace
A world where pain
And conflict will cease.

Eleanor Maddocks (12)
King Henry VIII School, Abergavenny

I Have A Dream

I dream of a world where there is peace and joy
I dream of a world where every child has a toy
I dream of a world where rivers are calm
I dream of a world where no animals come to harm

I dream of a world where skies are blue
I dream of a world, do you dream of one too?
I dream of a world where no one is blind
I dream of a world where everyone uses their mind

I dream of a world where there is no anger or fright
I dream of a world with courage and might
I dream of a world where no one cares about race
I dream of a world where people don't judge by face

I dream of a world which is friendly and fun
I dream of a world that listens to everyone
I dream of a world where there is no black and white
I dream of a world where it's safe in the night

I dream of a world where no one dies
I dream of a world where there is nothing to hide
I dream of a world where friends are forever
I dream of a world where couples stay together

I dream of a world where talent is shown
I dream of a world where rubbish is not thrown
I dream of a world where dreams become real
I dream of a world that has a beautiful feel

I dream of a world where disasters aren't around
I dream of a world where houses are not crushed to the ground
I dream of a world where diseases are cured
I dream of a world where African water is pure

If we want our dreams to be true
Let's give it a shot, just me and you.

Lauren Williams (11)
King Henry VIII School, Abergavenny

I Had A Dream

M y head hits the pillow as I fall fast asleep
Y et my mind is still racing

D reaming of men who gave up their lives to fight in a war
R unning from gunshots flying through the air
E very woman fears losing their man
A lump in my throat as the soldiers return home from duty
M y eyes open up and I realise it was a dream!

Jake Malnati (11)
King Henry VIII School, Abergavenny

I Had A Dream

I had a dream that I was a doctor
Curing and helping others
Being a wonderful person
Just think of me as a brother

I had a dream I was righteous
Doing what I should
Instead of mucking about
I really wished I could

No homework would be great
Wow, just playing around
With the TV on with a loud sound
I just wish I was never late

I had a dream I was still small
Then I wouldn't miss tiny rides
Curved in a little ball
Rolling from side to side

I had a dream I was the ruler of the world
Telling people what to do
Just sitting there in my chair
Saying to myself, 'Woohoo!'

Amin Idjer (12)
King Henry VIII School, Abergavenny

I Have A Dream

I have a dream that I could fly up to space
To planets and stars

I would fly there by rocket
Day and night
And when nightfall comes
Curl up tight

All the stars and planets
Surround me
Like a pack of wolves
Hunting

And when I lay there
At night on Mars
I could count all the stars
In the sky

I would look through my telescope
All day long
And watch
All the falling stars

And then one day
I'd come back down
With one.

Gareth Beavan (12)
King Henry VIII School, Abergavenny

I Have A Dream

I dreamt I was on a beach,
Well out of reach,
From the hustle and bustle of the town,
Which only makes me frown.
I long for lazy days under the sun's rays,
I dreamt of swimming in the sea,
Which would set me free,
From all the dirt and grime
And away from all the crime.
I dreamt I was laying on the sand,
Where I wouldn't lift a hand,
I need a resolution,
To solve the world's pollution,
I want to breathe fresh air
And feel the breeze in my hair.
I dreamt I was on a beach,
Well out of reach.

Alice Rose Jacob (12)
King Henry VIII School, Abergavenny

I Have A Dream

It's the 2012 Olympics
I'm in the British Judo team
I stand up and bow on the mats
As I hear the crowd scream.

I win my first fight
And then my second
I'm going really strong now
Until the final beckons.

I bow to my opponent
It is my final fight
One person will have victory
That is me tonight.

I step up on the podium
The British flag is raised
My gold medal around my neck
Wow! I am amazed!

Cassidy Skinner (14)
King Henry VIII School, Abergavenny

I Have A Dream

I have a dream,
That people are free from war and corruption
And that people can wake up in a bed,
Instead of a box.

I have a dream,
That people are treated fairly,
Regardless of the colour of their skin
And that a child can walk down a street without fear, or danger.

I have a dream,
That people can have medicine,
Regardless of their way of life
And that people can change the future,
Without damaging the present.

I have a dream,
A simple dream,
For world peace.

Gareth Bevan (14)
King Henry VIII School, Abergavenny

The Silent Pillow

As she sleeps there in her bed,
Thoughts escaping from her head,
Her inner secrets being freed,
Releasing her of her dirty deeds.

She speaks of them only to her silent pillow
And listens does that faithful pillow,
For he cannot speak
Of the deeds done that week.

She speaks of death, treachery and murder
And the pillow dares to say he heard her,
For, although he cannot speak,
The thought of deeds so bad makes him weep.

And when, in the morning, she awakes,
The silent, faithful pillow still quakes,
With the fear of what he heard that night,
But what will be heard tomorrow night?

When she returns with more restless dreams,
Of things that will make the poor pillow scream,
But he cannot speak
And has no tears to leak,
So what will become of this faithful pillow?

Melanie Boyd (14)
King Henry VIII School, Abergavenny

I Have A Dream

I have a dream
Actions speak louder than words
I have a dream
Inspiring others
I have a dream
Family and friends
I have a dream
Peace and war
I have a dream
Awake, asleep
I have a dream
Imagine, imagine, imagine
I have a dream
Love and hate
I have a dream
Voice in a crowd
I have a dream
Light and dark
I have a dream
The world itself
I have a dream
Here, there
I have a dream
Forgiving others
I have a dream
Rich and poor
I have a dream.

Stephanie Eadie (14)
King Henry VIII School, Abergavenny

I Have A Dream

I have a dream
That continues on
A never-ending one
It's me playing for Man Utd
Scoring goals galore
All one big adventure
Fans chanting my name
Being on the winning team
Playing next to pros
Lifting the trophy
Premiership top scorer
Player of the month
Everyone knows your name
Going abroad
On tour
Hosting teams
Signing autographs
Walking into the changing rooms
Having a laugh
Then I wake up to a boring old day.

Rhys Morgan (13)
King Henry VIII School, Abergavenny

I Have A Dream

I have a dream
To fly with the birds
Up in the air
Away
I have a dream
To have a pet mole
Who eats jelly
In a hole
I have a dream
To end world hunger
With loads of chocolate
And burgers
My dream is to swim
Swim in the sea
Swim to the bottom
With loads of seaweed
Then I wake up
Forget all about it
Get on with my life
Until next time.

Lewis Davies (13)
King Henry VIII School, Abergavenny

Magical Dreams

When will white see
Black as white?
When will peace win
The fight?

When will prejudice
Be gone?
When will evil just
Be wrong?

When will love rule
Over all?
When will terrorism
Fall?

What I want is just
To see
If all was good how
The world would be.

So I dreamt of peace
That night
Of how the love won
The fight.

I thought of all mankind
As friends
And that was when
My dream did end.

Catherine Eeles (12)
King Henry VIII School, Abergavenny

I Have A Dream

I have a dream to touch the moon
I have a dream to end all doom
I have a dream that flowers always bloom

He has a dream to end all poverty
He has a dream to mend all sadness
He has a dream to send help to the world

She has a dream to feed the world
She has a dream to lead the world
She has a dream to read and write

We have dreams for a perfect life
They have dreams to terrorise the world
They have dreams to cause men to hate
People have dreams, plenty of dreams.

Sophie Talbot (12)
King Henry VIII School, Abergavenny

I Have A Dream

I have a dream, a fantasy
Which I dream of almost every day
A perfect world
Free of hunger, thirst and despair
A world free of poverty
A world which hasn't heard the word 'war'
I know my dream
A perfect world is hard to achieve
But I inspire my dream
And cherish it every day
A planet full of happiness, joy and laughter
A place where everyone loves each other
A world full of beautiful green trees
From fast-flowing, deep blue rivers
To tiny silver streams
This is my dream, the dream I cherish every day
I wish from the bottom of my heart
That my dream would come true
Today or any day.

Kithma Welgama (14)
King Henry VIII School, Abergavenny

I Have A Dream

I have a dream

H appens almost every night
A nnoys me, it's a bad dream
V ery disturbing
E specially since it shows the future

A vision of the future

D estruction of the world
R ealising I must do something
E very day it comes nearer
A t least I know what will happen
M an will be destroyed by global warming.

Robert Murray (13)
King Henry VIII School, Abergavenny

I Have A Dream

My dream is to explore the world,
To go where no one else has been,
To see what no one else has seen,
This is my dream.

An archaeologist is what I'd like to be,
To dig up old things for the world to see,
How we lived in the past,
This is my dream.

My dream is to become a dancer,
To be seen by millions,
To earn billions,
These are my dreams.

Charis Lee (12)
King Henry VIII School, Abergavenny

I Have A Dream

I have a dream
A dream to find world peace
The dream which will make my wishes
Come true and be free.

For all the people in the world to be happy
What a lovely world that would be
For there to be no more wars
To settle old scores.

Not to kill animals just for the fur
To let them be and make them free
And let them live in harmony.

No more starvation in the world
Children dying, mothers crying
No more starvation in the world
What a dream this would be.

Lizzie Tavener (12)
King Henry VIII School, Abergavenny

I Have A Dream!

I stare, people stare back

H urrying to lesson, trying to avoid . . . them
A lone, scared, panicking . . . where are they?
V ery long corridors for me to face, no one likes me
E xpecting the worst . . . why me . . . why?

A day that's full of darkness and wonder

D reading what might happen and what might have happened
R ealising who they are and why they don't like me
E veryone knows . . . yet no one cares
A mad imagination, they're everywhere, even in my sleep
M y parents don't know . . . I want them to! I'm just too scared!

Bullying - speak up!

Kirsty Veitch (13)
King Henry VIII School, Abergavenny

I Have A Dream

I have a dream
A big dream
A dream that might come true

My dream is a secret
My dream is thoughtful
A dream that might come true

My dream is about peace
About no more hunger or suffering
A dream that might come true

My dream is a big dream
But I hope it can come true
So help me and help everyone around you.

Josh Evans (13)
King Henry VIII School, Abergavenny

I Have A Dream

I have a dream to change the world
To put an end to hunger and to war
I have a dream to change the world
To feed all children near and far
With clean, safe water that will go far
I have a dream to change the world
To make world peace in whatever shape or form
I have a dream to change the world.

Zoe Griffiths (13)
King Henry VIII School, Abergavenny

Dream

I have a dream to be a voice in a crowd
My voice so soft, but meaning so loud.

I have a dream to be right, not wrong
To always be here - proud and strong.

I have a dream for the world to respect, not hate
To save the important sources . . . before it's too late.

I have a dream that could never come true
To bring you back out of those doors you walked through.

I have a dream for us people to equally be as one
To equally think the same good opinions under the one same sun.

I have a dream for you and me
To not waste our world - that is the key.

I have a dream to change the world
For people to equally love the same and not to judge
By appearance or name.

I have a dream for my dreams to come true
To treat the people and world right
And to make the change - just to protect you.

Mercedes White (12)
King Henry VIII School, Abergavenny

I Have A Dream

I have a dream,
A very nice dream,
To sail around the world.

I have a dream,
A very exciting dream,
To fly over London in a hot air balloon.

I have a dream,
A very peaceful dream,
That all lies will be taken out of every soul.

I have a dream,
A very helpful dream,
To help all the people in need.

I have a dream,
A very hopeful dream,
To get a good job and carry on in life.

Levi Robinson (11)
King Henry VIII School, Abergavenny

I Have A Dream

I dream that one day
We'll all get along, I say
Black or white
Unintelligent or bright
I don't care if we have to pay.

I dream about world peace
No more arguments or wars, please
Get along with one another
Peace and love wouldn't you rather?
There is no such word as hate
We've all got to have faith
So stop groaning and whining
Because the day you do, the sun will start shining.

I dream of no lies
Not even cries
I dream of no more crimes if we may
When this stops, oh, what a happy day!

Don't give up on your dreams
It will come true as it seems
If you really hope and pray
It might come true one day.

Beatrice Kamau (12)
King Henry VIII School, Abergavenny

I Have A Dream

I have a dream to change the world,
A dream of no more war,
No more yelling, fighting or abuse,
No people getting badly treated because they are poor.

No more war
No more suffering

I have a dream to change the world,
A dream of people having a chance,
No more swearing, smoking or drugs,
No more people can pounce because . . .
There will be no . . .

Wealth
Or poverty
Just average people
In our safe world.

Jack Govier (12)
King Henry VIII School, Abergavenny

I Had A Dream

In my dream
There was no rubbish on the floor
No one here smoked
That was something more.

In my dream
All humans were fit and well
And of course
There were no bad things to tell.

In my dream
There were no burglars or crooks around
There wasn't any chewing gum
Or dog stuff on the ground.

In my dream
There were people that were all friends
All these things were good
Until the dream did end.

Rachel Jones (12)
King Henry VIII School, Abergavenny

I Have A Dream

I have a dream that the world has no wars or drugs
I have a dream that there are no diseases
And the only thing you can die from is old age
I have a dream that everyone is nice to each other
Not depending on what colour your skin is
Or what nationality you are
I have a dream where there is no hate, only love.

Nathan Holley (11)
King Henry VIII School, Abergavenny

I Have A Dream

I have a dream, a dream I say,
A dream, I dream almost every day,
It is of no war, fighting, suffering and much more,
They are all gone,
So the homeless have homes,
Animals live for years and freely roam,
The hungry have food and drink
And this is what I always think,
If it happened I'd be glad, but it hasn't, which makes me sad,
I have a dream, a dream I say,
A dream, I dream almost every day.

Aaron Marfell (12)
King Henry VIII School, Abergavenny

Inspiration

Inspired by a vet
I decided to get a pet.

Inspired by a choir
I decided to sing higher.

Inspired by a builder
I started to cut
For the poor people in Africa
I made a little hut.

Inspired by an artist
I decided to draw
So I sat on the floor
And drew some more.

Inspired by a person
I learned to talk
Inspired by a person
I learned to walk.

Inspired by my mum
I learned not to make fun.

Inspired by friends
I learned to have fun
Inspired by friends
I never play with a gun.

Maya Mossop (11)
King Henry VIII School, Abergavenny

I Have A Dream

A dream of a world with no war or hunger
A dream to fix an ever-expanding ozone layer
My dream is to cure all diseases that kill and maim
To stop global warming!
A dream that ceases rare and beautiful animals becoming extinct
A myriad of ideas in my sleep.

Harry Lesbirel (11)
King Henry VIII School, Abergavenny

With The Willpower

With the willpower
It would be good for me
With the willpower
I could lift up a tree

With the willpower
I would reach great heights
Like giving children better rights

But with the willpower
I could do better things
The world would be greater
The world of kings.

Rhys Willbourn (11)
King Henry VIII School, Abergavenny

I Have A Dream

I have a dream
That the lunch hour will be longer
So that the juvenile belly can properly digest
The wholesome and nutritious food.
I have a dream.

I have a dream
That the school day will be shorter
So that the mind of a child, like a tree stretching its branches
Will be more at ease for tests and homework.
I have a dream.

I have a dream
That teachers will not be allowed to shout
So that children's faces will not redden,
Ears, small, attentive and immature will not burn with shame
And doleful eyes, with long eyelashes, will not prickle.
I have a dream.

Sam Ellis (11)
King Henry VIII School, Abergavenny

My Dreams

My dream is to be a football star
And to play for a top club
Like the team I support, Manchester United,
But I am not good enough to play that standard of football.

I have another dream to be a famous sprinter
And I would go to the Olympics and win the gold medal
In all of my races,
But I am not fast enough to get there.

I have another dream to be a famous man
And for people to know me when they see me,
When I go everywhere around the world to see them,
But I can't do that, because I'm too shy to do that sort of thing.

I have another dream to play football,
For a team local to where I live,
But guess what? I can do that because I am still young
And I have plenty of time to think about my other dreams!

Ryan Price (11)
King Henry VIII School, Abergavenny

I Have A Dream . . .

About a world without famine, poverty or death
About a world where no one fights or quarrels
About a world where everyone agrees
I dream of a world where the people are in charge
Not one person.

Jack Wheatley (11)
King Henry VIII School, Abergavenny

I Have A Dream!

I have a dream
That all my dreams come true

I have a dream
That no one shouts or screams at each other too

I have a dream
Where actions speak louder than words

I have a dream
That you love me as much as I love you

I have a dream
That you light up my heart

I have a dream
That you are my light in the dark!

Cheri Jones (14)
King Henry VIII School, Abergavenny

My Dream

My dream is something that is big
My dream is something that is colourful
My dream is something that is round
My dream has a pot of gold at the end
My dream is to stand on a rainbow!

Sophie Smith (12)
King Henry VIII School, Abergavenny

I Have A Dream!

I had a dream
That one day we'd see
What a wonderful world
We have to be
To get everything that we wish
We have to stop being so childish
But as the years get older and older
We'll have to see if we
Get weaker or bolder.

Emma Parton-Wroe (12)
King Henry VIII School, Abergavenny

Dream

D eclare peace
R emove all weapons
E veryone at peace
A nouncements of peace given all over the world
M urders are no more.

Tom Fury (12)
King Henry VIII School, Abergavenny

The King's Agenda

Memories, such lovely things,
Go whizzing through the air.
Someday they'll lose them altogether,
But they don't seem to care.

One day they'll feel a stabbing woe,
Their hearts will wrench and tear.
They'll realise that, where something was,
Something isn't there.

My pen calls time a moving train,
With memories trapped inside.
I *need* to catch it up again,
I *need* to take the ride.

Every little drop of soul
And feeling do I capture.
For letters are my pride and joy
And writing is my rapture.

In hand I take my paper shield,
My pen shall be my sword.
The people will live their lives again,
At a price they *can* afford.

One day I met a hopeless king,
Death, he utmost feared.
When I asked him what was wrong,
In thought, he stroked his beard.

'I've lost my point in life,' he said,
'What's the point if there's nothing left after?'
This sounded such a silly fret,
But nobody gave in to laughter.

I considered, before leaping into the air,
I whispered, 'I have the conclusion!'
And of this turbulent conversation,
This was the phenomenal diffusion.

'There is a gift so wonderful,
But hard to understand;
It confirms that all your memories,
Are always close at hand.'

'This thing,' I said, most confidently,
'Is mightier than the sun,
It can catch the drop of evil in hate
And in love, the spark of fun.'

'So,' said the king, 'of what do you speak -
This weapon, this power, this . . . thing?
Can I possess such a curious item?
For it, two gold coins I bring.'

'Oh no,' I said, 'half a penny is all that I request
And I promise that anything I sell
Can only be the best!'

'So, what do I buy?' enquired the king
(Well, what do *you* think?)
Swiftly I did answer:
'I give you the miracle of . . .

. . . *Ink!*'

I saw the inspiration come;
A twinkle in his eye
And under the deep confusion
Unfolded a new mind as broad as the sky . . .

Isabel Anne Stokes (12)
King Henry VIII School, Abergavenny

Dream

D ream is what you do while you sleep
R eality is the world when you wake
E very dream is different
A nyone can have a dream
M any dreams are nice, but some are scary

At night while we are fast asleep
Into our minds a dream will creep
Long dreams, short dreams, dreams of fairies
Nice dreams, strange dreams, some are scary.

Antony Symonds (12)
King Henry VIII School, Abergavenny

I Wish I Could Fly

I wish I could fly
Fly far, far away
Away from war, hunger and poverty
Stop child abuse and killing
Fly from hatred and love
A place with peace and love.

David Fury (11)
King Henry VIII School, Abergavenny

I Have A Dream

I have a dream of a world without any war
I have a dream of a world where no one is poor
I have a dream of a world that's filled with love
This place of which I dream is like the Heaven above
And life in this world is a bit like a game
With nothing to lose but everything to gain
My view of this land is the land of the free
This is a world I would like to see
This is the world that Earth could be.

Ciaran Griffiths
King Henry VIII School, Abergavenny

I Have A Dream

My dream would be for peace
To stop us fighting and arguing
We will all be friends
It will be lovely on Earth
No wars or battles
But it is all a dream
And I hope it comes true.

Jayson Hollingworth (11)
King Henry VIII School, Abergavenny

I Have A Dream

I am a famous guitarist or an Olympic trampolinist

H ate does not exist
A ll illegal drugs do not exist
V iolence hardly ever happens
E veryone in the world is happy

A nimals are never killed for fun

D iseases do not exist
R acism does not exist
E veryone has agreed that there will be no more wars
A law says smoking is banned everywhere
M urder never happens.

Rachel Atkinson (12)
King Henry VIII School, Abergavenny

I Have A Dream

I have a dream
To go into politics
And make the government
Give lots of money to charity.

I have a dream
To make more campaigns
For children in need
All over the world.

I have a dream
To rid the world
Of gangsters.

I have a dream
To make the world
A lovely, peaceful place
Where nobody commits a crime.

Nicholas Davies (12)
King Henry VIII School, Abergavenny

Think

Think of a world where everyone is equal
Think of a world where peace is international
Think of a world where war is taboo.

Think of a world where all religions live in harmony
Think of a world where prejudice has vanished
Think of a world where love is the most common feeling.

Think of a world full of forgiveness, empty of revenge
Think of a world where all are cared for
Think of a world where Heaven is a place on Earth.

Just think!

Sophie Cashell (11)
King Henry VIII School, Abergavenny

I Have A Dream

D ream to swim with dolphins
  that's my dream
O f all the things I dream to do
  this is the best
L ove every minute
  that's what I'd do
P eople think it's a waste of money,
  but I think it's worth every penny
H ome to the beautiful dolphins is the big, deep blue sea
  that covers a large percentage of the Earth
I t has stuck with me
  since I was very little
N ot in captivity, a research centre is best
  where they swim almost freely in the ocean
S wimming with those great creatures
  is a huge ambition of mine.

Lydia Nicholas (12)
King Henry VIII School, Abergavenny

I Have A Dream

I have a dream
That all the wars will end and there is no pollution at all
I have a dream
That I will never argue with my sister because we never get our way
I have a dream
That abuse will stop and no one lives in silence
I have a dream
Do you?

Beth Davies
King Henry VIII School, Abergavenny

Dreams

I have many, many dreams
And one of those dreams
Is to one day fly to the moon
And dart in and out of the sparkling stars
That glisten in the dark sky!
Or maybe I'll become a star!
A star at riding
I'd love to be able
To fly over towering jumps
And conquer my fears!
To be able to save money
And keep it locked away
Safe from my spending temptations!
To get a good job when I'm older
And maybe, just maybe, become a millionaire!
But I'd love to spend time in sunny Australia
To see my family and swim in the sea!
I know I'd love to do something amazing
That no one has done before
And become famous!
But most of all
I never want to leave or lose my family!
Time will tell!

Catrin Menzies (11)
King Henry VIII School, Abergavenny

I Have A Dream

I have a dream
Of a world without racism
I have a dream
Of a world without terrorism
I have a dream
Of a world without sexism
I have a dream
Of a world where everyone is treated the same!

Naomi Williams (12)
King Henry VIII School, Abergavenny

I Have A Dream

I dream that there will be peace in this world
I wish no one would starve
I dream to be helpful when I am older
To help others make peace
I wish there was no violence
I think to myself, *why can't everyone get along?*
I dream that everyone is treated fairly
That's my dream and I hope someday it will come true!

Katie Brocklehurst (11)
King Henry VIII School, Abergavenny

I Have A Dream

I have a dream of no war
Of people working side by side
To help the needy ones, like in Africa
Because if we work side by side
We can put aside our differences
And people won't care if you
Are black or white, tall or short
I have a dream!

Kieran Lewis (12)
King Henry VIII School, Abergavenny

A Dream

Walking on stage for the very first time
I hear the crowd roar as I start to rhyme
The music is pumping
The crowd are jumping
I sing my ballad, reaching the chord
Head up high, facing the Lord
Now it's time to take a break
Only ten minutes, it should take
I'm back on stage for my very last song
Heart is pounding, nerves have gone
I thank the fans, who come from afar
That's my dream, being a rock star!

Ben Jones (11)
King Henry VIII School, Abergavenny

My World

My dream is to make the world like the world I pray for every day
My world is a beautiful place
My world is a place where there is enough food for everyone
My world is where everyone is sheltered from the rain,
The wind, the snow
My world is a place where it doesn't matter what colour,
Shape, size or culture you are, we are all equal
My world is a place where animals roam free until the day they die
My world is a happy, peaceful, war-free world
My world can become our world if certain people
Try their best to help.

Ella Parkinson (12)
King Henry VIII School, Abergavenny

I'm Searching

I'm searching for a place
Where people don't attack
People for the fun of it!

I'm searching for a place
Where people from other
Countries don't persuade people
In different countries
To bomb that place
That they're living in!

I'm searching for a place
Where people don't take hostages for a ransom
And their families make themselves sick worrying!

So ask yourself
Where is that place?

Josh Tavener (13)
King Henry VIII School, Abergavenny

I Have A Dream

I have a dream
A world with no hate
A world full of love
We're still not too late

Racism is non-existent
Evil is not here
No such thing as murder
Kindness is sincere

You can change the world
By the thoughtful things you do
Let us make a difference
And let the love shine through

Reach out and help all others
With sympathy abound
Let us make a change today
Let's share the love around

Let us all be friends
Let borders disappear
Let's do away with wars
Let's do away with fear.

Christopher McIndo (12)
King Henry VIII School, Abergavenny

Ellen MacArthur

Once, I had a dream to sail around the world
Breaking lots of records, winning lots of medals
A solo, long distance yachtswoman
In a boat, all by myself

In June 2000 I sailed the Kingfisher from Plymouth to Newport
It took me 14 days, 23 hours and 11 minutes
I returned to port to crowds of people clapping me well done
I felt so pleased and happy that I'd had so much fun

I tried to break the world record and achieved the best again
I had beaten the French sailor Francis Joyon's record for men
I received such applause when I jumped down from my yacht
I could not believe I had received such a yachting cup

It was announced that I was to be appointed
A Dame Commander of the Order of the British Empire
I am probably the youngest to receive such an honour
And all because I dreamt I would sail upon my yacht, Castorama.

Natalie Spence (12)
King Henry VIII School, Abergavenny

I Have A Dream

I have a dream
That people can fly like birds flying in the sky
I have a dream
That war will end and peace will reign
I have a dream
That I can reach the sky
I have a dream
That cars can fly above the sky
I have a dream
That I can move a mountain
I have a dream
That I can go to the moon and sing my song
I have a dream
That right will always win
I have a dream
That bad will always lose and good will always win
I have a dream
That hunger will end
I have a dream
That joy will come from above and love will never end
I have a dream that there will be no rich and poor
I have a dream
That people will care about nature
I have a dream
That people will learn how to love and care
I have a dream
That mankind will be equal
I have a dream
That children have the right to a good education
I have a dream
That someday all my dreams will come true.

John Paul Doruelo (12)
King Henry VIII School, Abergavenny

I Have A Dream

I have a dream that sickness will end
I have a dream that pollution will end
I have a dream that people will not do drugs
Or anything that will hurt their bodies
I have a dream that people will not hurt or kill other people

I have a dream that no one will make fun of each other
I have a dream that one day everyone will love each other
I have a dream that people will not pollute the Earth
I have a dream that everyone will live in peace

I have a dream that there are no more wars anywhere
I have a dream that there are no more fears and no tears
I have a dream that world hunger will end
I have a dream that money won't take over the world

I have a dream that people will be equal
I have a dream that my family will be rich someday
I have a dream that everyone can believe in themselves
I have a dream that people will respect me for who I am.

Geane Marie Delos Reyes (12)
King Henry VIII School, Abergavenny

I Have A Dream

I have a dream
To fly in the sky
To spread my feathered wings out
And flutter on by.

I have a dream
To have great powers
To turn bad things
Into flowers.

I have a dream
To go to an enchanted land
To see mystical creatures
That nobody has found.

I have a dream
To walk by the stream
And see little faces
Smiling at me.

I have a dream
A wonderful dream
That only I can see.

Elyse Holder (12)
King Henry VIII School, Abergavenny

I Have A Dream

I have a dream about becoming a superstar
In football or cricket
In cricket I'll be a batter or a bowler
In football I'll be a goalie or a defender
I have a dream.

I have a dream about flying
I'll soar through the air
With my eagle-like wings
Through forests and clouds and rivers as well
I have a dream.

I have a dream about being rich
With piles and piles of money
I'll live in a mansion
With a giant swimming pool
I have a dream.

I have lots of dreams!

Ryan Pugh (12)
King Henry VIII School, Abergavenny

I Have A Dream

I have a dream
That there is no crime
No shooting, no robbing
To waste people's time

I have a dream
That there is no war
And I will not stop
Until it's over for sure

I have a dream
That there's world peace
No bombs, no guns
No nukes to unleash

I have a dream
There's no drugs
On the streets
No people acting like thugs

I have a dream
That there are no fights
Or those horrible things
That happen at night.

Callum Tovey (11)
King Henry VIII School, Abergavenny

I Had A Dream

I had a dream
That the world
Was made of chocolate

I had a dream
The world was at peace
With no war

I had a dream
I was
A rock star

I had a dream
I had a dream
I had a dream!

Zoë Reynolds (11)
King Henry VIII School, Abergavenny

My Dream With The Stars

As I slip into dreamland
I think about the stars above
How they glisten in the moonlight
In colours silver, gold and white.

I can see the fast shooting stars
Going left to right;
I've never seen
Such a beautiful sight.

In the peaceful velvet night
They twinkle so bright
I wish I could be with them up in the sky
But I'm happy here watching them all night.

But now it's time
To say goodbye
But I'll dream about them
All through the night.

Annika Nilsson (12)
King Henry VIII School, Abergavenny

Dreams

Dame Kelly Holmes had a dream
To run to an Olympic gold,
Martin Luther King had a dream
To equalise black and white,
Mahatma Gandhi had a dream
For India to be independent,
Elizabeth Pankhurst had a dream
For women to vote
Bob Geldof had a dream
For poverty to end
I have a dream
I just don't know it yet!

Robert Stark (11)
King Henry VIII School, Abergavenny

I Had A Dream

I have a dream nearly every night
When my eyes are closed up tight
Sometimes they're good, sometimes they're bad
But this one was a sight.

I dreamt that I was happy
That I had beautiful long blonde hair
It seemed that absolutely nothing was wrong
And everyone took care.

I didn't have my fat round glasses
My eyes were a shiny green
I had my perfect smile and cheeky grin
The best you've ever seen.

I had all the friends I could wish for
Inviting me over for tea
All the boys kept giving me presents
Valentine's cards all for me.

I was excellent at my school work
I was top group in maths
I was brilliant at playing football
We would always win a match.

There were no girls or boys calling me names
No one telling me what to do
This was something no one could wish for
But was going to end soon.

I woke up, it was only a dream
I stood up and felt OK
And I had to get ready once again
For a horrible, normal day.

Katie Samuel (12)
King Henry VIII School, Abergavenny

I Have A Dream

I have a dream
Of an adventure across the sea . . .

I have a dream
Of a sunset blanketing the Earth . . .

I have a dream
That makes the world feel small . . .

I have a dream
That makes you forget about life . . .

I have a dream
I have a dream
I have a dream . . .

Gaydaa Ramadan (11)
King Henry VIII School, Abergavenny

I Have A Dream

I have a dream to travel to places
And see new faces
I have a dream to meet famous people
And climb a tall steeple
I have a dream that my mum will win the lottery
And buy expensive pottery
I have a dream to live in a big country house
Where there may be a little mouse
I have a dream to have a best friend
And to start a new trend
I have a dream to become a nurse
And make enough money to fill my purse
I have a dream that there is world peace
And that all of the wars in the world will cease.

Elinor Tuxworth-Jones (12)
King Henry VIII School, Abergavenny

I Have A Dream!

I have a dream
The world will live in peace
I have a dream
That all poverty will be released

I have a dream
That all children will be educated
I have a dream
That all hunger will be eradicated

I have a dream
That climate change can be corrected
I have a dream
That sensible people will be elected

I have a dream
That with effort from me and you
I have a dream
That this will all come true.

Melissa Edwards (11)
King Henry VIII School, Abergavenny

I Have A Dream

I have a dream that war will end,
I have a dream that the world will mend.

I have a dream that there is no crime,
Lurking around to waste people's time.

I have a dream that the world will not part,
I have a dream that we'll take this to heart.

I have a dream that the world can be free,
I have a dream that cruelty will flee.

I have a dream that things can be fine,
Not making me shiver right up my spine.

Adam Brown (12)
King Henry VIII School, Abergavenny

I Dreamed A Dream

I dreamed a dream, it came to me
One shining summer's day,
A whisper on the lilting breeze,
From a land so far away.

A land where famine is unknown,
The famished are no more,
When parched, fresh water wets their lips,
On this so far, distant shore.

No evil cries or worried thoughts,
The selfish, they have fled,
Friends are friends, no taunts or laughs,
Where only peace will ever tread.

Each day one wakes up with a smile,
No fear of conflict, nor war,
Outstretched hands will welcome in,
Any guests to every door.

For safety, one will fear not,
The streets are open to play,
Muffled screams and silent stabs,
Do not occur each day.

Come walk along this distant shore,
Along the sun-kissed beach,
Come, drink in peace and harmony,
That, which violence shall not breach.

Amy Bradley (13)
King Henry VIII School, Abergavenny

I Have Dreams

I have dreams
Of becoming an endurance rider.

I have dreams
Of owning a stunning endurance Arab.

I have dreams
That me and the Arab will understand each other.

I have dreams
Of crossing the finish line.

I have dreams
That I hope will come true.

Sarah Baynham (12)
King Henry VIII School, Abergavenny

I Have A Dream

I have a dream
To be scuba-diving!
Swimming under the sea
Swimming free!

I have a dream
To see the fish
Glowing in the dim sunlight
This is what I wish!

I have a dream
To see the seaweed
Flowing smoothly
Running with the reed.

Samantha Manolescue (11)
King Henry VIII School, Abergavenny

I Had A Dream

The bullet shocked you,
I'm sorry, did I wake you
From the dream that I had?
It's a shame that the rain burns
Otherwise we'd dance in it . . .
And you know how much I love bepop.

A cell-shaded nightmare,
New ways to play.
Another one of my retro dreams,
Old ways to say, 'I'll wait.'
Good things will come to those
And there's another great steal with seven seconds on the clock.

My eyes tell you I shot
And it's clear, now, that I do all of my own stunts.
So dare me to forget this
And statistics show that I will.
But it's my 'Ferris Bueller' day off, so I'll keep dreaming,
None the wiser, developmentally arrested and there are you.

Kelan Handley (17)
King Henry VIII School, Abergavenny

I Dream

I dreamt that the suffering in the world was over
But then woke up and it was still happening
I used to dream of a world without war
Racial discrimination, poverty or violence
But now I know that's not going to happen
So I stopped dreaming
Maybe if the government cared a little
Poverty could be over and wars wouldn't start
And maybe, just maybe, they wouldn't lie over
Why they go to war in the first place
But we all know that's not going to happen.

Jessica Indge (13)
King Henry VIII School, Abergavenny

My Dream

I had a dream,
People screaming,
Sirens sounding,
Warning us to evacuate.

Bombs exploding,
Outside noisy,
Inside quiet,
Mustn't move.

So afraid,
Shells are falling,
Men are dying,
Women and children left alone.

If only the wars would end,
What's that shouting,
Coming closer?
It's Mum waking me up for school!

Amy Rubbery (11)
King Henry VIII School, Abergavenny

The Nightmare

As darkness falls,
I close my eyes,
I fall asleep,
Beneath the starry skies.

My dreams come quickly
And as they do,
My heart beats faster
I'm scared, are you?

Can you see that man?
He's chasing me,
Arms around me so tightly,
'Please let me go.'

My heart beats faster,
I break into a sweat,
Pulling the quilt,
It's soaking wet.

He's holding me tightly,
I push and fight,
'Let me go!'
I scream into the night.

Then suddenly,
I am awake,
Shaking and pale,
My hands they shake.

'Mum!' I shout,
'Mum!' I call,
She's holding me,
My dreams, I have forgotten them all.

Luke Christopher Haworth (12)
King Henry VIII School, Abergavenny

I Have A Dream

I have a dream
To be a professional footballer
I wish to play for Liverpool
And I'll earn lots of money

I wish to have a family
A very caring family
And everyone lives in happiness
That's how I want my family to be

I have a dream
To have a big house in Spain
And one in Liverpool
And there I want to live

I have a dream
To be rich
I want to be a millionaire
That is my dream.

Ryan Paul Davies (11)
Ysgol Dyffryn Nantlle, Caernarfon

A Dream Of Hope And Health

I dream a dream,
A glorious dream,
A dream that's bright and fair.

I dream a dream,
A wonderful dream,
A dream of light and peace.

I dream a dream,
A fantastic dream,
A dream of equality and wealth.

I have a dream
It's the most heavenly dream,
A dream of power and awe.

My dream makes this world go round,
It turns it upside down.

My dream unites Heaven and Hell
And makes this Earth an amazing place.

My dream is a dream of courage and bravery,
That unites the entire human race.

I dream a dream,
That one day this world will be filled with hope and health.

Rhys William Paul Jones (16)
Ysgol Dyffryn Nantlle, Caernarfon

Dieter's Dream

I have a dream
And it's wrapped in moist whipped cream,
On the top, it is placed,
A red, bubbly gleam.

I have a dream,
A dirty little fling,
A massive custard cream,
That'll go down nicely with something fatty.

But for this I cannot wait,
The fat, the calories, the rich, rich cream,
It's because of this I must lose weight,
Oh, I do hope that this is just a dream!

Elis Davies (16)
Ysgol Dyffryn Nantlle, Caernarfon

I Have A Dream

I have a dream where time has gone by
Nothing has changed, for I am still the same
I live in a world where love will never die
But in the end, you are gone when autumn came.

In the blue moonlight, I think of you
Like the wolf I am, all will hear my cry
Hoping that the moon does not turn to scarlet hue
But I still see you in the pendant of the night sky.

All is as peace but the cold arrives, causing me to shiver
As I walk by, I stop to savour the sight
All the lights are now rippling in the river
And then I run like the fox and disappear into the night.

In this whole new world, nearly all are kind
I hope to hear the words of your song
There's never a time when love is blind
But if I stay . . . will it all go wrong?

I have a dream of a whole new world, a glorious time
A world where none shall steal, kill and destroy it all
A world whose duty to protect shall be mine
Those who cause suffering shall soon hear my call.

Come, we shall walk on the clouds
A paradise in the sky, who would have thought?
Where all can join in the crowds
But I stop and think, is this the place I have sought?

Now I stand face to the sea, thinking of you
I can hear the wind calling me to truth
I close my eyes and dream beneath the warmth of sky so blue
All the others grown older, I have kept my youth.

I have a dream of the long, long path I follow
To the new world, shining like a pearl upon us
Follow me, all the way, to the lands of tomorrow
Don't stop! Follow the path of light, we must!

Benjamin Archer (18)
Ysgol Dyffryn Nantlle, Caernarfon

I Have A Dream

I have a dream
To play for a football team
My favourite team
That is my dream.

They're red and white
They have fame
And they never get beaten
They're the best, that's my team.

They are the best
They are the team
They're Man U
That's my dream.

Carwyn Mowle (12)
Ysgol Dyffryn Nantlle, Caernarfon

I Have A Dream

I have a dream
It might come true,
I want the world to be happy,
Don't you?

To be a singer
That's my dream,
But I don't want
To be mean!

To have two kids,
As happy as can be
And of course,
Love my family

To live in a mansion,
To have a good job,
But I don't want
To be a snob!

I want to be happy
And have good mates
And one nice boyfriend
To take me on dates!

To be a singer of R'n'B,
To be rich and famous
And as beautiful
As can be.

I want to be happy,
Healthy and free
God, please make this happen
For me!

Lois Mererid Howel (12)
Ysgol Dyffryn Nantlle, Caernarfon

I Have A Dream

I have a dream
For my kids to be happy and healthy
I have a dream
To have good friends
I have a dream
To be happy with who I am.

I have a dream
To have loads of money
I have a dream
To have a big house
I have a dream
To have a house in Spain.

I have a dream
To have no exams
I have a dream
To have no bullies
I have a dream
To have a clean world with no rubbish anywhere.

I have a dream
To have a sports car
I have a dream
To have a healthy life
I have a dream
To be married with a caring husband.

Cara Hâf Thomas (11)
Ysgol Dyffryn Nantlle, Caernarfon

My Dream

My dream is to marry a boy from McFly
And my dream is to fly
And pass the birds in the sky
My dream is to be a primary school teacher
But I am scared, they might be like creatures

My dream would be to be rich with money
And I wish the world could be sunny
I have a dream to be a star
And have a fast silver car

My dream would be to have plenty of shops
But they won't sell ugly mops
My dream would be to stop the world's wars
And help poor people more.

Katie Louise Jones (11)
Ysgol Dyffryn Nantlle, Caernarfon

My Dream

I have a dream
That I'll be a star
And have a lovely, super car
That will take me very far.

I have a dream
That I'll work in a school
That is the one thing
That'll give me a pool.

Elin Williams (11)
Ysgol Dyffryn Nantlle, Caernarfon

The World For Everybody

I wonder how the world would be,
Without pollution, war or burglary?
My ideal world would be
A world with only one country.

Only once would be nice
It would be nice if everybody had rights,
No poverty, cancer, nobody dies
That's my ideal world, where nobody cries.

Danial Tomos Jones (12)
Ysgol Dyffryn Nantlle, Caernarfon

My Dream

I have a dream,
For my parents to marry.
I have a dream,
For everyone to have happiness in their lives.

I have a dream,
To meet the Welsh rugby team.
I have a dream,
To be famous.

I have a dream,
To be safe 24 hours a day.
I have a dream,
To be alright.

Amelia Stubbs (11)
Ysgol Dyffryn Nantlle, Caernarfon

I Have A Dream . . .

I dream that when I grow up,
I'll be strong and healthy,
I'll live in a big house
And be very wealthy.

I'd like a life of happiness,
With no fighting or crime,
Poverty to be history
And peace to be mine.

I'd love to live on a farm
And drive a big tractor
And never having to go
To the doctor!

I'd love to have a swimming pool
And drive a car that's really *cool!*
A shiny red Ferrari
Or a silver Subaru.

I'd like to be a footballer
And play for Man U
And if I'm good enough
I'll play for Wales too!

I wish that my dream
Could one day be . . .
No longer a dream
But *reality!*

Rhodri Dwyfor Parry (12)
Ysgol Dyffryn Nantlle, Caernarfon

My Dream!

My dream is for everybody to be loved
For everybody to have a friend
A school and good health.

Say no to war
Say no to death
I just can't stand it!

I would like to see the world as one
With no countries or religion
Just plain fun!

Ffion Llewelyn Owen (11)
Ysgol Dyffryn Nantlle, Caernarfon

My Dream

Imagine a world without politics,
Imagine how it would be!
For everyone to be equal
And treated just like me.

My dream has no war!
And religions would be no more
And everyone would share
And then that would show we really care.

Imagine a world without fear,
Where no one would have to shed a tear.
Where animals were free to roam
And everyone has a safe home.

Perhaps one day we will see,
Where exactly we've gone wrong
And then if we can make ourselves do it,
We will unite and be strong.

Arian Hamilton (12)
Ysgol Dyffryn Nantlle, Caernarfon

My Dream

My dream is to have
A sports car
And a big house.

My dream is to work
With the ambulance
Or to play rugby for Wales.

My dream is for everybody
To have their own mum and dad
And everybody to be good, not bad.

My dream is for nobody
To be left out at the side of the road
And every country to have
A whole load of food and water.

My dream is to have no exams
And no bullies and everybody
To be friends and to be happy.

Alaw Medi Hughes (12)
Ysgol Dyffryn Nantlle, Caernarfon

My Dream

I wonder what the world would be
Without crooks and murderers and guns.

This is how my ideal world would be
With no wars and no army.

I dream that all the poor countries
Will have food, that poverty will stop
And everyone will be safe.

I wonder what the world would be
Without crooks, murderers and guns.

Gordon Lee Davies (11)
Ysgol Dyffryn Nantlle, Caernarfon

I Have A Dream

I have a dream
To be happy and safe
To have caring friends
I have a dream.

I have a dream
To be a hairdresser
Or a nurse
I have a dream.

I have a dream
For no wars
No religion
I have a dream.

Shannon Marie Daly-Bishop (11)
Ysgol Dyffryn Nantlle, Caernarfon

I Have A Dream

I have a dream
That's personal to me
To stop poverty, religion and war
To bring peace to the world and more.

Obviously, it is impossible
For a girl like me
To change the world of jealousy
Spite, ungratefulness, evil and poverty.

I would like to become successful
To become a real surgeon
Go all the way to Africa and help and educate
The children that have to survive through hunger.

How may I change the world?
Not by myself, but with help
How may I get world peace and no religion?
So people won't quarrel, who's right or who's wrong?

Yes, I do have a dream
It is impossible
Unless people decide to help this world
To change it for the better.

I have a dream . . .

Caryl Angharad Roberts (12)
Ysgol Dyffryn Nantlle, Caernarfon

My Dream

My dream is to have
Family and to be
A footballer's wife.

My dream is to pass my driving test
And have no exams in any school.

My dream is to breed
A champion bull terrier
So I can show it.

My dream is to live in Florida
And swim with the dolphins every day.

Nikita Roberts (11)
Ysgol Dyffryn Nantlle, Caernarfon

I Have A Dream

I have a dream
That my kids
Grow up
And have friends
Who care for them.

I have a dream
I wish it will come true
A want a horse
The one for me.

I want the most precious baby
That I've ever seen
She'll smile so sweet.

I want a family
That care for me
Stop the war
No fighting back.

Sara Owen (12)
Ysgol Dyffryn Nantlle, Caernarfon

I Have A Dream

I have a dream
That everyone will be friends
And I catch loads of bream.

I have a dream
That there will be enough food
For everyone.

I have a dream
That there is freedom for every religion
And different skin-coloured person.

I have a dream
That the world will be one
And I have a motorcycle.

Shane Broda (11)
Ysgol Dyffryn Nantlle, Caernarfon

My Dream!

My dream is to be a pop star
And for everyone to have enough money
And a big house full of happiness,
To be shared and have loads of friends
And to help stop the global warming
And to have a world with no fighting
And no violence.

Shauna Marie Jones (11)
Ysgol Dyffryn Nantlle, Caernarfon

I Have A Dream

I have a dream
That the picture on the wall,
Is a picture of happiness,
A picture of courage.

The picture on the wall
Lights up a dark world,
That is the picture,
That is my dream.

The picture of friendship,
The picture of love,
The picture on the wall,
Is the picture of dreams.

The picture of colour,
The picture of depth,
Is a picture of hope,
A picture of strength.

I've seen the picture,
I've seen my dream,
The picture of happiness,
The picture of trust.

I have a dream,
That the picture on the wall,
Is a picture of me!

Dafydd Wyn Jones (17)
Ysgol Dyffryn Nantlle, Caernarfon

I Have A Dream

I have a dream,
That catches your heart,
That makes you want to fly,
It will take hold of your fantasy
And set your spirits high.

My dream is how my future will be,
Full of hope and peace on Earth,
With no wars or violence or worries,
Only happiness that will fill my world.

I dream that I will be happy
And all my family and friends,
My dream is what I believe in,
My dream is what sets me apart.

I have a dream that is full of emotion and surprise,
My hopes and fears collide,
While I keep my dream inside of me,
It will catch my prayers and thoughts.

My faith is what will keep me strong
And will make my heart so proud,
My heroes will all be able to see,
My heart's desires come true for me.

My dream is of a world that no one ever sees,
Where there's happiness all year round,
Where the violence and pain and suffering,
Have all vanished before my eyes.

My dream is what I seek inside,
My dream is who I am,
It's what I will always hope for,
It's what I'll always hope to find,
My dream will forever be mine.

Nicola Leanne Hughes-Evans (17)
Ysgol Dyffryn Nantlle, Caernarfon

I Have A Dream

I have a dream,
That the clouds will be lined with silver
And the sun is lined with gold,
I have a dream,
That our blades will be blunt
And our ears will listen.

I have a dream,
That the rivers of blood will cease
And the rivers of knowledge will flow,
I have a dream,
That people will stop,
Stop everything just to hear.

I have a dream,
That people will fall
And the world will be soft,
The sharp corners will vanish,
Along with their sharp tongues.

I have a dream,
So do thousands of others,
We can hope and pray,
But will it come to pass?

Lucy Taylor (17)
Ysgol Dyffryn Nantlle, Caernarfon

I Have A Dream

I have a dream,
That one day there won't be gore,
I have a dream,
That there won't be war,
I have a dream,
The world full of life,
I have a dream,
The world without fighting
I have a dream,
The world without sorrow,
I have a dream,
There will be a better tomorrow.

Alun Jones (13)
Ysgol Dyffryn Nantlle, Caernarfon

I Have A Dream

I have a dream,
Peace will come to stay,
The world will be full of laughter,
No war, no crime,
Only peace and joy,
No war, no crime.

I have a dream
That all will be peace,
It will last forever,
Peace, peace,
That's all we want,
I have a dream of peace.

Anthony Morris (12)
Ysgol Dyffryn Nantlle, Caernarfon

I Have A Dream

I have a dream
That the sun will sing in harmony
And the clouds will dance with happiness,
That the world will be filled with joy and laughter,
With no violence, poverty or disaster,
So let us all be generous and kind
And make the world a colourful place,
We shall make it clear
That none of us should fear,
All I'm asking for
Is to stop this horrible war!
This is our wish, our dream,
Let's make it a reality!

Lisa Taylor (12)
Ysgol Dyffryn Nantlle, Caernarfon

Equal

I have a dream,
That the world is equal,
No one is different,
Black and white people are equal,
They can sit with each other
And share a flat,
No one will turn up their nose,
No more will be killed,
I have a dream today,
For everyone to be treated the same,
So please, help stop the pain.

Kerry Vaughan Wilson (12)
Ysgol Dyffryn Nantlle, Caernarfon

I Have A Dream

I have a dream
To rule the world
I have a dream
To have a perfect world
I have a dream
Nobody kills
I have a dream
Nobody dies
I have a dream
That the world will turn square
I have a dream
Liverpool are the best football team
I have a dream
To live in Wales
Forever!

Gareth Dafydd Evans (12)
Ysgol Dyffryn Nantlle, Caernarfon

I Have A Dream

I have a dream
To go out and scream,
I have a dream
To go out and laugh with friends.

I have a dream
That people can be friends
I have a dream
I hope the wars will stop.

I have a dream
There will be no bullying
I have a dream
No racism and fighting.

I have a dream.

Lia Wyn Williams (12)
Ysgol Dyffryn Nantlle, Caernarfon

I Have A Dream

It would be better for it to stop
Racism
Bullying
Sickness and the lot
But it won't stop
So we must stop dreaming.

It would be a perfect world
Happiness
Liveliness
That would be a perfect world for me!

Anna Louise Roberts (12)
Ysgol Dyffryn Nantlle, Caernarfon

I Have A Dream

I have a dream
To rule the world,
I have a dream
To make it perfect
I have a dream
For the world to live in perfect harmony
And always care for others
Full of happiness, peace and respect,
For the war to end and for there to be no violence,
I have a dream
For everyone to be generous to each other,
For the world to be safe,
For the world to be full
Of loving friends and family,
I have a dream
For the perfect world.

Lucy Jane Hawksworth (12)
Ysgol Dyffryn Nantlle, Caernarfon

I Have A Dream

I have a dream . . .
That all the racism will stop
There will be no fear.

I have a dream . . .
That no one will die
And no one will cry.

I have a dream . . .
That I will be the queen
And the best angel ever.

I have a dream . . .
That all my family
Will join me for dinner.

Lindsey Louise Jones (13)
Ysgol Dyffryn Nantlle, Caernarfon

I Have A Dream

I have a dream that someday
The world will be perfect,
No rape, no crime, no war,
No bullying, no racism, no violence.

A perfect world would be
A perfect world for me,
Safety, a future for everyone, peace, happiness, respect
And a life for everyone.

That's my perfect world
And maybe
You are not quite like me.

Anna Wyn Jones (12)
Ysgol Dyffryn Nantlle, Caernarfon

The Perfect World

The perfect world is with no racism
There will be no fear of others
No abuse to children
Or people killed for pleasure
Or for another religion

No children suffocated to death
No poverty, everyone living an equal life
No innocent person camping on the street
No one having to steal to live

In my perfect world no one will die
Or cry for any reason
In my perfect world everyone has a chance
Of an education
And every child has a chance to go to school

That's my perfect world
What do you think shall happen?

Alaw Jones (12)
Ysgol Dyffryn Nantlle, Caernarfon

I Dream

I dream of a world
Where the sky is purple,
With candyfloss clouds,
Where the trees are sugarcanes
And the grass is lollipops.

I dream that the world is a playground,
Where swings hang from the clouds
And the trees are slides.

A world without rules,
A world full of laughter,
No need to fear,
No need to cry.

I dream the water is honey,
That fills you full of sweetness.
I dream that the rain is gumdrops,
That fill the world with colour.
I dream the flowers can sing,
A song of rejoice.

My world is not a world of nightmares,
But a world full of dreams!

Ruth Victoria Hodgson (14)
Ysgol Dyffryn Nantlle, Caernarfon

I Have A Dream

Comments here, comments there,
But verbal abuse is everywhere.
Bullies throwing their victims from post to post,
With all his mates, they're laughing as he grins and boasts.
Fat or thin,
Short or tall,
None of that matters, not at all.

All of it's racism,
Verbal or physical, it hurts just the same,
But to all these sick people out there,
It's all just a game!

I have a dream too,
To make this world a better place,
For me and you.

Ryan Anthony Jones (12)
Ysgol Dyffryn Nantlle, Caernarfon

I Have A Dream

I have a dream that one day violence will be over
No fighting in the pubs
No fighting in the streets.
I have a dream that one day war will be over
No guns, no bombs.
I have a dream that the world will be a better place
No racism, no greed.
I have a dream that there will be no pollution in the air
No rubbish in the sea.
I have a dream, but it might not happen
That global warming is not happening.

Yasmine Liptrot (12)
Ysgol Dyffryn Nantlle, Caernarfon

I Have A Dream

Not being able to go out,
Not being able to go home,
Where can I be safe?
I don't want to feel scared,
All I want is peace,
Why can't people be happy and not argue?
Why can't they get on like before?
Why do they have to fight?
All I want is a happy family,
All I want is peace,
Please help me now,
Don't let it be too late.

Rebecca Ann Parry (13)
Ysgol Dyffryn Nantlle, Caernarfon

I Have A Dream

I have a dream,
That everyone will be happy,
No starvation,
No hearts torn,
No weapons,
No violence,
No one will suffer in silence.

I have a dream,
That no one will be greedy
And everyone gives money and food to people who need it
No animals will be extinct,
They have feelings too
If you think.

Maxeene May Hughes (13)
Ysgol Dyffryn Nantlle, Caernarfon

One Shot

One shot is all that it takes for success
In a world of many different dreams;
The world of fearful competition and gutless
People shown by their actions. Their powerful mind beams,
Which stray from one being to another create
A torturous atmosphere and this is today's world
I have a dream for friendships between each life, it's not hate
But is pride and belief that together they can form a bold
Connection through each soul and mind
To create a better life for the next generation;
My dream of seeing criminals and the cowardly people behind
The actions of death and torture would see the powerful connection
Between heavenly people and deeply regret not to be one and shine,
As they are now quarantined from the heavenly life and are now
Joined with the torturous and hated life from the people in their prime.
You only get one shot to take your chance and show
But the opportunity only comes once in a lifetime.
One shot is all that it takes to shine.

Adam Gordon Bee (16)
Ysgol Dyffryn Nantlle, Caernarfon